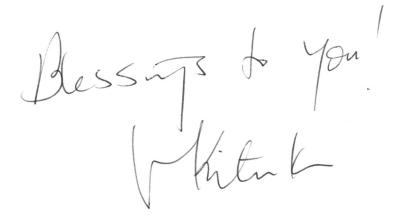

Blessings to you!

OVERCOMING BUFFALOES

At Work & In Life

OVERCOMING BUFFALOES

At Work & In Life

What You Need to Increase Productivity,
Overcome Setbacks and Stay Motivated
Without Leaving Your Life Behind

Dr. Vincent Muli Wa Kituku

To my mother,
Margaret Kasiva Kituku,
for bringing me up with
African folktales, hope, and work ethics.
Mama, you still inspire me
in a special way.

Contents

CONTENTS

Acknowledgments

To attempt to say thank you to each and everyone that has
helped, in any way, to bring this book into fruition
is just that — an attempt.

Divine Providence continues to amaze me with
His mightiness and the wonders of His love. I am blessed
with a family that is uniquely the source of my inspiration
and the classroom through which major life lessons
present themselves.

Special thanks to Kathy McIntosh, Rebecca Evans,
and Lynette Whiting for working on raw drafts and
making suggestions that have made this book readable.
Thank you, Lindsie Taylor, for the creativity you have
brought into my writing with your skills as portrayed
on the cover and layout design.

Audiences of my presentations and readers of the columns
I write have inspired me in ways words can't express.
Thank you ALL.

*"We are what we repeatedly do.
Excellence, then, is not an act, but a habit."*

ARISTOTLE

Living with Buffaloes

"Aaauuuiiii ... Uuuiiii ... Aume nakuu, muyuke mboo nino!"
This was a common cry in my native community. It was a "911 call" from Kamba women and means, "Men! Wherever you are ... here is a water buffalo in our village."

Near Kangundo, Kenya, where I grew up, were mountains that had a game reserve. From that game reserve, once in a while, a water buffalo would go astray. The water buffalo came without warning.

When there was a buffalo in the village, life changed completely. The first time I heard women screaming, it was because there was a buffalo in the village. I remember the first time I visited a person in a hospital. He had been stampeded upon by a water buffalo. I saw a lion trying to climb a tree to escape from a buffalo in a Discovery Presentation. A single lion would never dare to attack a mature water buffalo. It takes a pack of four to five lions between six and eight hours to kill a buffalo.

The water buffalo is a very stubborn and clever animal. Traditional stories had it that if you tried to climb a tree the buffalo would come and graze beneath the tree, waiting for you to climb down. If you took long, the buffalo, I've heard, would urinate on its tail and splash the urine on you (by chance, I think). The urine caused an itching effect on your body. Then you would scratch and scratch until you let go of the branch and you fell down from the tree to meet with the buffalo.

One could not escape from the buffalo.

In life, there are "social buffaloes." Any aspect of life that destabilizes progress in spiritual growth, professional development or harmony in relationships could be viewed as a "social buffalo."

Challenges at work, such as being laid-off, passed over for a promotion, or having a cruel boss could be compared to a buffalo encounter.

Challenges in life, such as divorce, feeling like a failure, or a betrayal by loved ones could be compared to the appearance of water buffaloes in an African village.

Buffaloes invaded villages without warning, devastating social structures, uprooting the harmonious livelihood of villagers and leaving them feeling insecure and stressed.

This book has the tools you need to overcome "buffaloes" at work and in life on a consistent basis and make success a lifestyle and a choice.

CHAPTER I

Have Something to Live For

*The worst poverty is not lack of material possessions
but the lack of dreams.*

I am told of the house I was born in. It was a small, circular
hut with walls of vegetation materials, mud and a roof of grass.
The house that is vivid in my mind was built in 1965. When it
was first built, I shared this somewhat rectangular two-bedroom
and one living room structure with my parents and three siblings.
Four other siblings were born there. To create space for the new
arrivals and provide my sister some privacy, my brother and I used
the living room as our bedroom.

Our family shared this habitat with other species. The moment
we opened the door, we were intruders in the rats' domain. They
stampeded all over as they scurried for cover. When their num-
bers were no longer bearable, my mother scheduled rat-reduction
days. This was an episode to remember. Hot water was poured in
one end of the rat holes by one of us while the rest waited with
militant readiness at the other hole with one mission to accomplish: Kill rats as they ran from the hot water. "Muli! There, one
is there, get it!" my mother or my siblings would scream at me. I
had the reputation for being the sharp striker.

Our home was also the residence for rat predators, snakes
and blood-sucking ticks. We kept our drinking water in a clay
pot that was positioned in one corner of the living room. This
corner served as a cool haven for snakes as they waited patiently
for their prey. Sometimes, when there was little water in the pot,

and one had to tilt it in order to scoop water with a calabash or cup, a snake would sneak up its head looking for whomever was in its territory. The presence of a snake brought everything else to a standstill. It had to be eliminated. One serpent dared to crawl over my mother's legs when she was on her knees praying her Rosary. When it finally left her, she called me, but she had taken care of the snake with a piece of wood by the time I arrived with a rock.

Ticks seemed less dangerous and easy to combat. My brother, Kisingu, had only one job...to pour water on the floor and thus make it harder for the ticks to jump. I would be the last to advocate for unwarranted destruction of natural resources. Ours was a matter of survival.

It was in this home that I learned "You can live with less if you have something to live for." Hard work and school were a priority in our home. My hard-working father set up a small shop selling clothes, food stuffs and other items Kangundo folks would buy. He demanded to find us reading when he came home at night. I remember him admonishing us on the importance of education in our future.

By 1979, the year I dismantled our structure which by then served as a kitchen, Dad had transformed thoughts of a better future into a fenced compound with nine bedrooms, a water fountain and two sons in higher institutes of learning. He is a living example of the future that a person with vision, determination, and hard work can have regardless of the dismal resources available.

You must have something to live for if you want to make your future better than your past and present.

CHAPTER 2

Be the CEO of All You Do

"A man only begins to be a man
when he ceases to whine and revile..."
JAMES ALLEN

If you are not in charge of your life, someone else is. And if someone else is in charge of your life, when will you take full responsibility for your life, grow and enjoy the tremendous benefits of being in charge?

One of the Top 45 Must Know Lessons for Top Achievers that I put together (now a top selling inspirational resource) states, "Always know that you are the CEO of all you do." To be precise, this quote is lesson number 12 in that list.

When you are the CEO of all you do, you are in charge of every aspect of your life that no one else can do for you. That includes, but is not limited to, your attitude, faith, health, recreation, professional and personal growth, and financial stability.

You are responsible for your family's well-being; you are involved in your family members' activities. It is your job to encourage each individual to live up to his or her potential.

You think and act as the owner of whatever you do. If you are employed, you forget job descriptions and do what adds value to the overall success of your organization. You constantly find ways to add value, whether in product development or in customer service.

As the CEO of all you do, you serve other people, whether paying clients or not, to the best of your ability, knowing that, "whatever you do for yourself can get you by. What you do for others is what gets you ahead; whether in your profession or personal or spiritual pursuits," as I stated in the Top 45 Lessons referred to above.

You surround yourself with achievers — people who challenge, inspire and support you to pursue whatever positive endeavors your life desires.

As the CEO of all you do, you learn to accept criticism and setbacks so that you can grow and do what critics thought you couldn't. You learn to leave yesterday's disappointments behind so as to concentrate on today's challenges.

As the CEO of all you do, you get involved in your community because the quality of your community's life depends on how committed you are to making it the best place for you and the people you love the most to live in.

CHAPTER 3

Born to Succeed

"We all have ability. The difference is how we use it."

STEVIE WONDER

Born to succeed was the thought that wouldn't leave my mind as my wife and I were discussing growing up in Kangundo, Kenya. We were brainstorming on what name would fit my wife's new child care and education center. We realized that the backbone of our professional and personal lives was rooted in what our parents, teachers and elders instilled in our young minds during our childhood — that we were born to succeed.

Like all children growing up in our community, we never had manufactured toys. We got clay from riverbanks and created our toys — cars, dolls, houses and whatever else we could conceive. With dry corn stalks I created mock spectacles. Our soccer balls were made of salvaged newspapers or torn cloth — the balls never bounced but we played with them. We played with mud. I made my first watch with a piece of paper and a bottle-top. Our world of fun and exploration was not limited by what we didn't have.

I remember part of my early schooling when our classroom was primarily under a tree. We learned to write our ABC's and 123's on the ground. If the wind blew, our homework was gone. I still recall the rainy days that led to unexpected no-school days — natural holidays.

Later in school, there were no textbooks for the pupils. Teachers wrote what we were to learn on the blackboard and erased it at the end of a period. Songs were also written on the board for a short period of time and we memorized them for life. However, even with the myriad of challenges, we were taught life lessons that transcend classroom walls.

Learning was part of life — not isolated for five days a week. What comes to mind is the day my mother taught me the multiplication table as we were putting manure in our garden. That has not been erased from my memory in the more than 40 years since it happened. Years later, I used a family activity to teach one of my children the multiplication table. Since then, she has never had challenges in that line of arithmetic.

Several teachers sacrificed their Saturday mornings to come to school and help us prepare for the extremely difficult high school entrance exams. They were not paid overtime. Their greatest reward was to see the young people in their community succeed. There were other adults who were not relatives or our teachers who still encouraged us to do our best, not only in school, but in life.

There was a woman I didn't know who spanked me when she found me and my buddies hiding, sneaking out to try a cigarette a "friend" had, from my sixth grade class. A principal from a different school took time to tell me that using my time to study was a better investment than helping at a small restaurant my father owned.

Looking back, it's hard not to highlight key factors that were critical in our upbringing.

Parents, teachers and other adults believed in us. They all contributed to prepare us for the unpredictable future. They cared. We were told family stories (among others) that helped us know who we were and gave us the sense of belonging each person needs. We learned stories of traditional heroes and their struggles and triumphs against stronger forces.

We learned that respect is not slavery — we gave our seats to adults and listened without interrupting when someone else was talking. We shared any book available. We were responsible for bringing clay or whatever else teachers needed for our learning. Lack of material goods was never considered poverty. Improvisation was part of life...and that's how you succeed.

CHAPTER 4

What's Your "ZOOP?"
Be Creative

"You can have brilliant ideas, but if you can't get them across, your ideas won't get you anywhere."
LEE IACOCCA

The product ZOOP, from the Denver Zoo, represents creativity at its best. ZOOP is nothing but manure made from animal droppings at the Denver Zoo. It is dung! Information on the three-pound container says that "ZOOP is an exotic manure-based compost produced from the waste of conscientious recycling-minded animals residing at the Denver Zoo." The cost for three pounds of ZOOP is about $10 and when you add shipping and handling, you are paying approximately $20.

I first heard about ZOOP from Mark Sanborn, CSP, CPAE. I just had to hold it, own it and keep it in my office as a constant reminder that all one needs to thrive in any endeavor is creativity. Suffice it to say, creativity need not even come up with something new, but can find new uses for whatever is already available.

As a native of Kenya, the world's premier home of wildlife, I couldn't help but think of one fact: some portion of ZOOP is from exotic animals originating in African lands millions call home. However, I never made a dime from wild animal manure.

Looking at ZOOP from another perspective, I realized I am a seasoned backyard gardener who for years has bought steer manure (don't ask me why they call it steer manure, not bull or cow manure), about 20-30 pounds at a time, for $1.99. Yet three pounds of ZOOP cost a whopping $10.

Creativity, in this case, is packaging an existing item in a way people will purchase (at a premium price) out of curiosity (in my situation), emotional attachment, or pure ignorance. Manure from any herbivore will most likely give you the same results, whether from a cow, moose, or impala. Manure is manure. What differentiates ZOOP from the rest, in my opinion, is how it's presented with an angle to increase its perceived value. It is a small package with a simple appealing marketing pitch: "100% ORGANIC... MADE FROM THE GENEROUS CONTRIBUTIONS OF THE ANIMALS AT THE DENVER ZOO." Another section reads, "A LITTLE ZOOP GOES A LONG WAY."

Do you have an idea, skill, talent or product that can be presented to people in a new form? It is astonishing how people get rewarded for turning ordinary items into products people want to buy. Animal dung anywhere is still animal dung; yet ZOOP is capturing people's attention. At least it captured mine!

What can you do with what you already have?

Are the resources (skills, talents, and experiences) that you already have being used in the most rewarding manner?

If not, what can you do about it?

What are you waiting for?

ZOOP reminds us of the old wisdom that mashed potatoes anywhere are still mashed potatoes. What people change is the gravy. Add the best "gravy" to whatever resources you have and begin your journey of fulfilling endeavors.

CHAPTER 5

Never Ignore Unexpected Opportunities

There is a short story about a man who was traveling through a vast desert. After several days, he ran out of water and food with no human dwellings in sight. Thirsty, tired, and with hunger almost claiming his life, he came to a spot where a poor-looking desert dweller was selling ties. This traveler pleaded for food and water while the desert man tried to sell him a tie. The traveler insisted that all he cared for was a drink and a meal and continued his journey without a tie.

A few hours later he saw a place that had trees and buildings. As he came close to the area, he saw the green watered lawns. He smelled food. Then he saw people entering a building that appeared to be a restaurant and decided to go to the same building. At the gate, he was informed that nobody was allowed to enter the restaurant without a tie.

Think of how Sacajawea became a key player in the expedition of Lewis and Clark. I don't recall if historians indicated that Lewis or Clark had planned to meet and include a young Native American Indian girl from the Shoshone tribe as a member of their expedition. Yet Sacajawea is credited for their survival and the preservation of their diaries.

So the question is:
Could there be opportunities that you have ignored because you are so focused on your vision that you can't see what you need to make your vision materialize?

Are there resources that you have ignored because, like the tie, they don't seem relevant for your immediate need?

Around 1993, I had determined that I would one day help millions of people as a professional communicator and writer. I had been a scientist all my adult life. I casually shared my vision with a neighbor whose job was delivering milk with a factory truck.

The following evening, I had a knock on my door — it was my neighbor. All he said was, "Vince, here. This book might help you with what you want to do with your life. I have had it for years but I think you will use it." It was Napoleon Hill's bestselling *Think and Grow Rich*. I had never heard of it — it's still among the best books I have ever read.

Unexpected opportunities, when recognized and put to work, have a way of positively surprising the world.

Toastmasters, the organization that provides people the opportunity and resources to be better public speakers, was the tie along my path that catapulted my professional and personal life beyond my wildest dreams.

CHAPTER 6

You Must Believe in the Future You Expect

"If one advances confidently in the direction of his dreams, and endeavors to live the life which he has imagined, he will meet with great success unexpected in common hours."
HENRY DAVID THOREAU

They say a picture is worth a thousand words — one photo with four of my high school classmates in 1978 speaks volumes. For years I have had sadness whenever I see that photo.

It isn't easy to write this story. My inspiration to do so comes from the knowledge that an untold story can be a constant source of agony. When we don't tell a story we deny our fellow travelers an opportunity to acquire an aspect of life that might be all they need to reach their stars.

We were in Form IV (high school senior) students of Tala High School in Kenya — the place I consider my utmost stepping-stone for both academic endeavors and personal awareness.

Not every student in Form IV was guaranteed admission to the next level. Over 80 percent of the students never made it. The struggles to achieve the required grades for admission in what was called Advanced Level, a two year school before another terminating exam that only a few (less than 5 percent) managed to pass and get admitted to the University, were phenomenal.

Our academic challenges at Tala High were compounded with the fact that we had to perform adult responsibilities. We lived in rented apartments. Sometimes up to six students shared a one room apartment. We advised ourselves on when to study. We fetched water, shopped for our food, hand-washed our clothes, cooked our meals and managed the meager budget from what little our parents gave us for survival.

We had been studying as a group of five buddies when another student with a camera stopped by. We seized the moment and wanted memorial photos taken. One of us said we should point at the direction of Nairobi University. That was our vision. That is why we were hitting the books.

We kneeled down, each on one knee. We all faced the direction of Nairobi University with the exception of one student **who did not point at the direction of Nairobi.** The rest of us did.

That hurts me to this day. **He was the only one, out of the five, not to achieve the required grades for the next level.** Three of us eventually lived our vision. The fourth friend who pointed with us passed the exams with flying colors but decided to get employed and help his family.

The student who didn't point was a close friend of mine. We had been together in primary school. After I noticed that he had not pointed at our ultimate goal, I asked him, "Why?" He said something that indicated he didn't believe he could make it. That left me with the burden of figuring what had gone wrong. He had been an academic giant. I had struggled my entire elementary school years, spending SIX years in three grades. His performance in the high school entrance exam was superior. But four years later, he had lost the fire that comes with self-belief.

Do you believe in your capability? If you don't, then know you don't have a vision. It is written, "Without a vision, people perish." A vision cushioned by self-belief inspires creativity that is never limited by available resources. It fuels determination that knows no boundaries.

CHAPTER 7

Vision: The Crucible for Purpose and Destiny

"The most pathetic person in the world is someone who has sight but has no vision."

HELEN KELLER

I can only speak or write of what gave me, a previously recognized underperforming student, the hope to know I could make it to Nairobi University.

What gave me the courage to publicly indicate that I believed I was heading to that coveted institute of higher learning where less than 10 percent of high school students were admitted?

It was a vision imprinted on my mind by a simple action of my father. In January 1975, the results of the high school admission were released. My brother and I had scored acceptable grades. Yet, what our father did thereafter changed my life forever.

He took us to the gates of the University of Nairobi and said, **"My children, that is where men and women come to get knives to cut their portion of the national cake."**

Those words were and still remain the greatest call to action that I have ever heard.

Some background knowledge is necessary for you to understand the impact of those words in my life. I had spent six years in three primary school grades. My father had spanked me until my lack of improvement made him give up the ritual that he performed whenever I brought my mediocre grades home.

That past was eternally changed with a vision of going,

"...where men and women get knives to cut their portion of the national cake." It gave me a clear picture of the life I could have regardless of the academic abilities I had portrayed. It gave something to look up to beyond the high school years. It created a sense of purpose that has a specific destiny.

It has been said that, **"hard work beats talent when talent is not working hard."**

I opened and kept my books open. It is hard to recall more than two or three days that ever passed without opening a book. During holidays, I used to hide in one of my primary school classrooms to study, either what we had learned in class or what was to be covered. I gravitated toward classmates who were academic sharp shooters.

Looking back, that vision, impressed on a high school-bound mind, became the road map I needed for a future that was not yet thoroughly envisioned.

I now know and believe that without that vision, it would have been next to impossible to succeed given the devastating experiences that I (and my family) went through. I removed my sister's drowned body from a river in August 1975, a year after my brother died of measles. My grandfather died a year later followed by the death of my last dog a week later. My father married, divorced and re-married three times. In my father's territory all wives and their children lived in the same house, cooked and ate from the same tray—a life experience that is better left for eternal healing. My uncle, who was a grade ahead of me in high school and with whom I shared an apartment, and my closest friend each destroyed their lives with alcohol and drugs.

- Vision provides hope and challenges people to do more with their potential.

- Vision is the crucible needed for a life of purpose.

- Vision provides focus.

- When people have a vision, their creativity, efforts and resources are devoted toward an expected outcome.

- Vision helps people avoid distractions and seize opportunities they would hardly notice without an established goal.

- When people commit to turning their vision into reality, they grow — whether spiritually, mentally or professionally.

- With a vision, people become the CEO of their own attitude, decisions and action. They become accountable for their own destiny.

CHAPTER 8

Plant in the Dry Season

*Unspectacular preparation is the springboard
of outstanding performance.*

In Kangundo, Kenya, there are two seasons — rainy and dry. Farmers plow and plant corn during the dry season when the soil is loose and easy to turn. With the corn seeds in the ground, farmers know their crop will germinate when rain falls. Planting in the dry season also ensures that the corn seeds are not unearthed by squirrels because it impossible for them to tell which spots have seeds and which do not when the soil is dry.

This metaphor applies to many aspects of life. When we do things because we are forced to, it is like planting after the rain falls. The soil is heavy, and "social squirrels" may interfere with our progress. Anxiety, panic or illness may set in and curtail our success.

This also applies to today's unpredictable workplace. Career changes brought by downsizing, business mergers, technological advances, deregulation and fewer restrictions on international trade regulation have become part of our lives. To survive and thrive in the present turbulent workplace, one has to prepare with foresight rather than hindsight. Chance favors those who are prepared. Luck is the product of preparedness and opportunity. It is easier to learn the skills for your next position while you are at ease with your current one. Crops that germinate shortly after rainfall are planted in the dry season.

If you repair your roof when it is sunny, you won't have to worry about getting wet while trying to do it in rain. The future depends on the sacrifice you make today. Plant when the "soil" is loose, and "social squirrels" are unable to unearth your efforts.

Are you planting in the dry season for whatever call or mission you have in this world?

If not, what is stopping you?

CHAPTER 9

Push Your "AC"

"Inaction breeds doubt and fear. Action breeds confidence and courage. If you want to conquer fear, do not sit home and think about it. Go out and get busy."

DALE CARNEGIE

I learned in high school physics class in my native Kenya that "AC" meant alternating current. In 1986, I came to Wyoming for my graduate program at the University of Wyoming and bought a car. It had a button that was marked "AC." I did not dare to touch that button!

One hot summer, we drove from Laramie, Wyoming to Portland, Oregon and back with seven people in the car. We improvised ways of keeping cool. We opened the windows, stopped regularly and used hand-held fans.

Later, while riding with my family on a hot summer day, our friend Sandra Biegzube asked why the air conditioner was not on. "Our car has no air conditioner," I replied. She pointed at the "AC" button and pressed it.

Relief had been at our fingertips all the time!

Do you have a talent, gift, experience or resource (air conditioners of some sort) that you are not using?

Is there something you have always wanted to do but you have been afraid to try?

Millions of talents and gifts come and go from this world packaged within people who never used them. Yet, when you use a hidden talent, you increase your productivity and motivation and improve your sense of purpose.

Many factors stop us from pressing the "buttons" of spiritual, professional or personal growth.

1. **Loyalty to the past.** If I had not learned that "AC" meant alternating current, I probably would have tried to find out what that button was used for. Past experiences, especially failures, may be a hindrance to progress. A key to success is to try and try again after failure. A spider web is destroyed by other insects over and over again. But the spider keeps trying until the web is completed, even if it is completed in another location.

2. **Loyalty to others.** Fear of appearing stupid has caused thousands of spiritual and social buttons to remain unpressed. What would others say if you did something unexpected? Successful artists present the world as they see it themselves, not what they think others see.

3. **Fear of the unknown.** Fear of the unknown is worse than fear of certain pain. I have heard it said that if people were to put their worst misfortunes into a common basket and then choose whichever misfortune they wanted from that basket, each person would choose his own. To the Israelites, going back to Egypt, the land of bondage, seemed better than the talk of the Promised Land. This factor has kept people in situations they hate, abusive associations, destructive habits and spiritual stagnation. Remember, although the ship is safe at the harbor, and it is less likely to be damaged by storms, it was not made to stay at the safe harbor.

4. **Self-devaluation.** Avoid focusing on what you think you do not have instead of what you have. If you will take a minute and list the resources you have for the life you envision, you will be surprised to discover that you already have a resource that can get you started in any venture.

5. **Looking for success "out there."** Trying to find meaning, fulfillment, worth and identity in a career that you dislike, in unprofitable associations, or in habits that are detrimental to yourself or others is like trying to improvise a cooling system. You have what it takes to live a fulfilling life.

CHAPTER 10

Avoid Suffering from "African Impala Syndrome"

"Make the most of today — translate your good intentions into actual deeds."

GRENVILLE KLEISER

Over 80 percent of adults don't live up to their greatness because they suffer from what I call "African Impala Syndrome."

Jumping high and forward is an inborn talent for survival of the African impala. The impala is known to jump about ten feet high. This high jump propels the impala to land about thirty feet from the spot where it starts. With this ability of vertical and horizontal jumping, the impala survives and thrives in the carnivore-infested savannas of Africa.

However, the impala has a unique limitation. It jumps only when it can see where it will land. I once read from an issue of "Bits and Pieces" that when the African impala is confined by a three-foot-high fence, it won't jump.

As I think of the African impala, I often wonder how we fail to live up to our potential because we suffer from "African Impala Syndrome." We don't "jump" unless we can see "where we will land."

The symptoms of the African Impala Syndrome can look like some of the following:

• Staying in situations that may be stressful, even harmful to our mind, body and soul.

- Holding on to habits that we know may be detrimental to our growth.
- Not trying new projects because we may not see what the results may be.

We lack the faith needed to move forward. How do we get the faith back?

1. To jump forward, you have to use the word **BUT** cautiously. **"BUT"** is a "wall" that nips talents before they can blossom. When your life is governed by **"BUTS,"** chances are that your talents, gifts, and experiences are underutilized.

2. Understand that your not "jumping" not only hurts you, but all those who could benefit from your jumping. If you, as a parent or boss, go back to school, chances are that your children or employees will emulate your example.

3. To "jump" from your current state that you don't like or wouldn't like to be in five years from now, you only need permission from one person — YOU. Take inventory of what resources (people and material goods) you need to help you launch your "jump."

4. Faith is a dynamic condition of mind through which desires, plans or goals are translated into tangible results. The first step of putting your faith in action is to determine your desire and purpose. The second is to pursue it no matter what obstacles you face.

5. Once you have developed a goal, keep negative thoughts like failure, fear, anger, and envy from your mind. Associate with people who will encourage you. Acknowledge that for every step backward, there is one or more steps forward that bring you closer to your goals.

6. As you jump by faith toward your determined goal, never let a day pass without doing something related to your goal. Surround yourself with materials that are in tune with the goal you want to achieve. Always remember, the power of belief makes the difference.

7. Remember, when we "jump," we may suffer pain or failure. However, it is a tragedy for you to never live up to your potential because you didn't jump. By not jumping, you may avoid pain or the experience of failure. But you won't learn, change, or experience self-love and growth. And the pain from being stuck in your situation and the regret that you did nothing about it when you could is more scathing. Only by jumping can we liberate ourselves and others to jump higher and further.

8. If you are waiting for inspiration in order to jump, you are a waiter.

9. St. Augustine said, "God has promised forgiveness for your repentance, but He has not promised tomorrow for your procrastination."

Whether You Are a Lion or Gazelle: Run!

"Regret for things we did can be tempered by time; it is regret for things we did not do that is inconsolable."

SYDNEY J. HARRIS

There are some life lessons in the way animals survive and thrive in the jungle that can teach us to "survive and thrive" in our own jungle – our workplace. Studies suggest that a person will have changed jobs seven to nine times between ages 18 and 35. If you own a business, you are going to experience unpredictable challenges.

How can you survive competition?

Can your skills, knowledge and ability keep you marketable?

In the jungle, life is just like that – uncertain. Both carnivores and their prey are faced with the challenge. The challenge is running either for food or from being food.

To capture the picture of life in the jungle, read what the wise have said:

"Every morning in Africa, a gazelle wakes up. It knows it must run faster than the fastest lion or it will die. Every morning in Africa, a lion wakes up. It knows it must run faster than the slowest gazelle or it will starve to death. It doesn't matter whether you are a lion or a gazelle; when the sun comes up, you'd better be running."

What can we learn from both the lion and the gazelle to survive and thrive and grow in our profession, spiritual pursuits or in our relationships?

Here are some tips to run with:

1. **Identify the nature of your "jungle."** What is happening in your industry, now and tomorrow? What professional and personal attributes do you want to improve as you strive to attain new heights? What are the opportunities within your immediate reach and the ones you can explore with time?

2. **Don't run aimlessly.** Gazelles run from carnivores. Treat anything that limits you from living up to your potential as a "carnivore." You can run from poverty, mediocre performance, and an inability to build and maintain relationships with God and fellow human beings by developing a purpose to live. A lion identifies a target, positions itself and then the running begins.

   What is your target in your professional endeavors? What is your target in your spiritual pursuits? What kind of relationship do you think is good for you at home and in your community?

3. **Concentration.** Imagine what would happen to a gazelle running from a lion that engages in other activities not related to surviving. Or to a lion that decides to run after every available gazelle. Lions are known for strategic hunting. A lion focuses on one target and nothing else. It applies the law of discrimination against anything that is not of relevant importance as it runs after its goal.

4. **Determination.** As they run for food or from being food, animals have to overcome obstacles — bad terrain, thorny bushes. Determination is what keeps them from being a victim — food for a lion or a starving lion. Personal fulfillment in life bears a deep meaning when we remember the obstacles we have to overcome through our determination.

5. **Association.** Jungle animals survive together. Lions hunt together, sometimes in packs of four to five to bring down a water buffalo. In our jungle we have to have associates we can work with and depend on.

6. **Know when you are safe.** Either from your predator, if you are a gazelle or with your meal, if you are a lion. This is directly related to having a specific goal. A gazelle cannot run for the whole day...it has to know when it is safe and then use its time grazing, feeding a baby or socializing. Same with a lion — when it has its kill, that's success. How will you know you have achieved your goal?

7. **Know what to do when you are not "running."** Hone your skills, abilities and knowledge. In today's jungle, learning-to-learn is an asset. Learn to expand and integrate your knowledge, communication skills, thinking and reasoning skills, and interpersonal skills.

8. **Never give up.** A lion may change its course or target, but never gives up. No one will ever know you had a goal to achieve if you give up. You may adjust your strategies or the nature of your goal — but never give up.

CHAPTER 12

Succeeding Without Extraordinary Talents

"Vincent, when the Boise State football team gets on the field, they know why they are there and what they have to do to succeed." This was said by a former BSU football coach as we discussed the presentations I had given to his deeply talented team compared to other teams in the Western Athletic Conference (WAC).

One clarification: talent has its place in life and people who are talented and use their talents well do succeed in extraordinary ways. What I want to make clear is that you can succeed in what you do even if you don't have talents.

I had given numerous motivational speeches and training sessions for both players and coaches at BSU since 1998. After the above statement, I started paying attention to the key aspects of individuals that required no talent, but led to enormous success in professional and personal endeavors.

My involvement with the BSU football team has been one of the greatest experiences in my life. Why would it not be for a Kenyan who comes to the United States with zero football knowledge, then reads about it in newspapers and asks a coach to let him speak to the team about winning, focus, teamwork, staying away from drugs and other destructive off-the-field activities?

Today, I am probably the only human being with several coaches' uniforms (from several schools) for a sport I had no clue how it was played when I first spoke to the BSU team. Allow me to add that in 2003, after the team won several conference championships and bowl games, I was honored by being selected as their Grand Marshall for the Homecoming game.

However, what intrigues me is the performance level of the BSU football team, year after year. The WAC teams don't have deep pockets to compete for talent against upscale football teams. But Boise State football players have what individuals need to succeed in life even if they don't have noticeable talents.

1. **Passion to learn.** In 2002, the team had just won the conference championship when one of the players said, *"Even champions can get better"* as they prepared for a bowl game.

   The players on this team are teachable. You stand in front, and you can see and feel how they are sucking in every bit of wisdom or practical tip you share. You don't need talents to be teachable. What you need is a desire to learn, discipline and to apply learned information.

2. **Ability to learn from all available sources.** How many coaches out there would risk having someone who had no clue how football is played speak to their team?

   "Even though you never played football, your understanding of how a team must function as one to be successful is amazingly accurate," wrote Dirk Koetter, Arizona State football head coach after one of my presentations.

   The tips you need for something that is dear to you may come from unexpected sources.

3. **Invest in growth.** When last did you attend a seminar or read a book that was not required for your job?

   When last did you take someone you want to learn from out for breakfast or dinner?

In football, time matters in a huge way. To have someone come speak for an hour is a huge investment. You need to invest in your mental, physical, and spiritual growth.

4. **Self-initiative.** This comes with extra trimmings...responsibility for one's choices, decisions and actions, and putting a plan together for achieving one's goals. You would be impressed to see young men in their late teens and early twenties doing what needs to be done without being asked to. No talent is ever needed to be self-motivated and to do what needs to be done before one is asked.

5. **Flexibility.** What talent do you need to change?
   Some of the players had excelled in certain positions while in high school. However, for their own growth and the team's success, they learned knew skills for different positions. Change is the currency that will buy you a portion of the future in a world that is changing faster than ever before. No talent needed.

6. **Courage to try.** I worked with the team several times before I learned who was who and how they had joined the team. Brock Forsey, an outstanding player, was a walk-on — a player who was not recruited and had no scholarship but the coaches allowed him to join the team after they watched a demo video. Brock was one of the best players the school has ever had. Millions never live up to their potential because they lack the courage to walk-on into potential opportunities.

7. **Steering away from distractions.** There is no talent needed to stay away from habits and activities that take your focus

and efforts from what you love. This starts with the associates you keep. To succeed you need to have people around you who are positively investing in their own futures.

8. **Persistence.** Our youngest child's name means persistence. No talent, education, money or family connections are needed for one to be persistent.

   Is your goal important to you? Does it help you live a better life? Then why quit?

9. **Be humble.** While I have seen these players in team meetings, I rarely recognize them when they come to the classes I teach at BSU. They just blend in with other students. Humility requires no talent.

CHAPTER 13

Own Whatever You Do

"Forget about likes and dislikes. They are of no consequence. Just do what must be done. This may not be happiness, but it is greatness."
GEORGE BERNARD SHAW.

Just before Florida's Hurricane Charley, there was a message posted on an Internet site in August 2004 by a Florida resident. The message was, *"As long as it leaves the power on at my house but knocks it out for a few days at work, I'll be fine."* It is disturbing to know there are people who wish the worst to their employer or place of employment. It is even more disturbing to think that you work for somebody else.

Has the thought ever come to you that you don't leave your home to go and make anyone else rich or that you don't work to pay anyone else's bills?

The primary reason we work for payment is to cater to our own needs and wants. Someone else may provide the projects for you to work on, the place to do them and write a check to you for your time, energy, and creativity. But we work on the projects knowing that there will be a payment for us.

A story is told of some villagers who hated their chief. They complained that he asked them to do a lot and demanded that each family give his stores a portion of their harvest. Some contributed as little as they could because the chief seemed to have other important matters to care for instead of monitoring what each family brought. This attitude of working while complaining went on for several years. Then one day their community was attacked by enemies and all the villagers ran to the chief's compound where he had shelters.

To the surprise of the villagers, they found that the stores had different sections with names for each family where the chief's servants stored whatever portion of the harvest a family brought. When all the villagers were in the shelters, the chief announced that he had learned from his advisors that the village would be under siege for about two weeks. He then gave a directive that each family should use what they had contributed to survive for the two weeks — and no sharing with others.

The complainers, who thought they were working for the chief and storing food for his family, were in for a shock.

The first step in owning what you do is to find something good to think, and talk about it daily, beside the paycheck.

If you can't find anything good about what you do, you are stealing from yourself. You will probably stress about it and try to sabotage efforts for progress, even sometimes your own progress. You have to find something about what you do that gets you excited.

You have to learn to see how what you do contributes to the bottom line of your workplace.

Do you have skills that are currently not used, skills that you could use to improve customer service or the productivity of your workplace?

You may want to investigate how to become an active contributor (one who is aware of his organization's vision, matches it with his own and does whatever is necessary to bring success for himself and the organization).

To grow your skills and knowledge, you have to use them where you are. Waiting for the future to develop yourself and to turn your growth into tangible returns is a self-defeating strategy. What is not used is generally lost.

To thrive in unpredictable workplaces, you need to prepare yourself for tomorrow today. You need to understand growth is a byproduct of completing daily tasks and routines in various manners. What will make you the best is your ability to use and pass your knowledge and skills to others. Serve without reservations.

You will have the cutting edge if you know how to get the best from other people by listening, teaching, observing, empowering, developing others and treating others with the respect they deserve. For that to happen, the best employees know that they must be open to different views, build trust, encourage others, add value to other people's lives and consider others first.

You must value inspired decisions and actions based on the vision you have for your mission in this world. That is different from forced decisions and actions — the things you do against your heart's desire.

CHAPTER 14

Don't Kill Yourself with Instant Success

You have heard stories of people who win the lottery only to have their lives dive into lows worth leaving alone. You have read what happened to many of the winners we saw rush to huge dollars and then seem to disappear into oblivion — Miss Universe or high school sports stars who left high school to earn unfathomable millions.

Each of the so many sad endings evokes one of my childhood observations that has refused to free itself from my memory. We lived in Kangundo, Kenya, a relatively high potential area with enough rain to support livestock from season to season. Another area, Yatta, was drier and rain was unpredictable. Livestock owners would keep their animals in Yatta as long as they could and hope for rain. When their animals' condition was pathetic and the hope for rains diminished, the owners opted to take them to areas where there was grass and water.

Watching a newly arrived animal eat, drink and die taught me more than any seminar or class. The cow from the drier area just ate whatever it could. When full, the next thing it did was walk to the river and drink as much as it could. Cows rest after eating and drinking before continuing to eat. Unfortunately some of those animals never got up from their rest — they died there — killed by what was supposed to make their life better.

The general animal physiology explanation is that the animal in poor condition eats more than its digestive system can handle. The undigested build-up produces acid that gets into the blood, gets transported to the brain and kills the animal.

The astonishing part of death from instant success is that it can be avoided. Look at the people serving meals in famine-stricken communities. The servers don't just serve whatever is available and in whatever quantities. They start with light meals in portions the digestive system can handle considering the condition of the people. The food, amount and form, is adjusted as the body condition improves. Thousands of people are saved.

Did you know there are great professionals who would have continued enjoying what they did if only they didn't have instant success in the beginning? Their instant success destroyed their motivation and focus, or brought pride that always precedes a fall.

This leads us to some basic wisdom. Enjoy the hardships of your growth — the rejections from publishers, the prospects who don't return phone calls or email messages, the challenges of lacking the resources you need to get to the next level or the less than spectacular results you are getting from your weight loss efforts.

The dues of hardship that you pay in your learning process might largely be the parameters that will prevent you from "social death" from instant success — since yours won't be instant success. The long-term efforts one devotes in achieving professional and personal successes are what make their success sweet.

CHAPTER 15

An Attitude of Gratitude

*"Gratitude is not only the greatest of virtues,
but it is the parent of all others."*

CICERO

For six years, I wondered whether God had designated Laramie, Wyoming, as a testing zone for winter misery. I arrived on the 10th of February, 1986. It was a cold winter morning. The temperature must have been below anyone's survival level, or at least that is what I thought. Welcome to Wyoming! When I left Nairobi, Kenya, on the 7th, the temperature was in the 100s.

They told me in Wyoming that I should expect two seasons, the 4th of July and winter. My friend Rodney told me that snow could be expected during any month except July. The snow problem was always amplified by wind. The speed of the wind was phenomenal. There was no need for raking and bagging leaves in the fall. Wyoming winds blew them to Nebraska or Colorado.

I disliked the winter conditions of Wyoming and looked forward to the day I would leave. On the 6th of April, 1992, I started to work on an ecological project for Idaho Power Co., which generates its electricity mainly by use of water power. The main source of the water is snow. Indeed my very livelihood depended on snow. Soon, I joined the others at Idaho Power in praying for snow, especially given that there had been snow scarcity for about six years prior to my coming. The decorations on the Christmas tree that year were centered on one theme: Let It Snow! Let It Snow!

The forest fires of 1993 covered the Treasure Valley with smoke, and the air was stifling. Migraine headaches became a problem, thus prompting me to wish for the Wyoming winds. If only we had some of the wind in Wyoming, I wouldn't have migraine headaches.

Thus I learned to appreciate and be thankful in any situation. Perhaps it is 8 a.m. on Monday or a rainy day that ruins fishing, shopping, or golfing plans. Maybe somebody else's prayers are being answered by the conditions we think are making our lives uncomfortable. The list of things to be grateful for is endless in every situation.

Often, our attitude of gratitude is impaired by the fact that we focus on the "storms" in our lives. We only see the desert we are traveling through. However, there is always a rainbow behind the cloud and a stream in the desert. When we keep our eyes and hearts on the rainbow and the stream, we maintain an attitude of gratitude. We thank God despite the prevailing circumstance.

At times, the rainbows and streams seem not to be there at all. Actually, we just don't see them. This is where family, friends, and associates help us.

No one can be ordered to have an attitude of gratitude. However, it is contagious. It can flow naturally from parents to children and from friends to friends. We can cultivate an attitude of gratitude by being thankful for our daily portion of fresh air, unpolluted water and three meals a day, shelter, freedom, health, jobs, opportunities to be creative, and chances to enrich the world with our uniqueness.

Attitude is determined by how we respond to experiences. It is how we react to incidents, not the incidents themselves, which determines our attitude. We have little control, if any, over natural forces like tornados, earthquakes, floods, disasters, illness, and pain. What really matters is our internal response systems. How we respond to these calamities is something each individual can control.

Life is difficult at times and easy at other times. Tranquility depends on how we respond to difficult times.

CHAPTER 16

Pillow Menu
A Perspective on Life

Are you blessed with a pillow?

Is it the right kind of pillow that meets your sleeping expectations?

Do you have a back-up pillow should you decide to turn or lie on your back in the middle of the night?

Are your pressure points resting on a pillow that provides assurance that they will function tomorrow?

Until recently, at a five star hotel where I saw a Pillow Menu, a pillow to me was a bedding item whose main purpose was, and still remains, to keep someone's head in a raised position at night. If a pillow is not available you can use your hand!

What if you sleep on your side? No problem. *Firm Synthetic* is the pillow for you, a "firm, fiber fill pillow" that "gives you supreme support."

If you are a back or stomach sleeper, *Medium Down* is what you need. The description says, "be cradled in the feathery support of plush down."

Those who alternate sleeping on their sides and back should use a *Firm Down* for "both support and the luxurious feel of down filling."

The last, but not least, entrée is the *U-shaped neck pillow.* The attraction for this is to "relax pressure points for a night of well-deserved rest with this neck support pillow."

The above Pillow Menu, with the nature of the different kinds of pillows and what each is supposed to accomplish, was on one of the beds God (the provider of good things) and my clients (who pay the bills) have made it possible for me to sleep on at some hotels. I couldn't help but let my memories take me to my childhood days. It was a life of limited options.

As I reflected on life in Kangundo, Kenya in the '60s and early '70s, I remembered two kinds of soaps, Kivanga and Toyo. Those were used for bathing and washing clothes if you couldn't afford the floury Omo, the detergent that helped dirt dissolve easily from our heavily soiled clothes. Kivanga or Toyo were used as substitutes for the rarely available body lotion, petroleum jelly.

Matu ma mukondo — Solanum leaves are what we used to wash our dishes. Those leaves were the ultimate grease buster.

Before the luxury of choosing the kind of pillow that suits any sleeping position I unconsciously choose *was* introduced to me, I paid close attention to what had replaced the only two bars of soap I grew up knowing about. I reserve the right to not attempt to list the numerous detergents we use to wash our clothes. If you live in the United States (or any industrial nation, for that matter), chances are that your main challenge is to purchase a detergent based on your desires, but not because it's the only choice.

Here is my morning routine. I start with a facial soap followed by a before-shave cream. When I toss the disposable razor blade, the next step is applying after-shave cream before smearing my whole face with a facial lotion (a Mary Kay beauty product) my wife tells me is for keeping my face looking youthful!

Then the hair has its own shampoo and conditioner. The various shampoos come in different containers at Costco and so do the many types of body lotions. The toes have two chemicals for keeping fungi controlled. The sole has lotion for maintaining its softness. Spare me the agony of explaining what each of these potions does. One piece of wisdom a married man learns is to "do what you are told by your wife and use what she gives you."

Those pillows brought a lump to my throat. A bed made of ropes and a mattress of cow's hide can and does make a night long. Some Saturdays were dedicated to eradicating ticks from a bed-resembling structure. Going to high school meant having a mattress of a three inch thickness that we used on a foldable bed whose front part lifted a bit — thus making a portion of the mattress a substitute pillow.

Just look at the extras in your life and you can't help but say, "God, I deeply thank you for your goodness."

CHAPTER 17

The Third Degree of Thankfulness

The first scribbled piece resembles a star and the words next to it are, "You are the star of my life."

Another demonstrative drawing has the following text next to it: "With your big smile you make my heart feel nice and warm. You are like a father to me...!"

The note ends with a, "Thank you Vincent!!!"

A heartwarming message, captured in a letter filled with drawings all held together by three ribbons — this is one of my most precious possessions at the moment.

When Alex handed her token of gratitude to me, she had no idea that she had taken my life to another realm of spiritual experience. The humble experience of being appreciated by a girl 11 years old, a stranger I had met through her grandmother, gave my life a new meaning — experiencing the third degree of thankfulness.

What we are familiar with is being thankful for our health, family or a job and other blessings that are bestowed on us. That is the first degree of thankfulness. Most of us would agree that these are some of the reasons we are thankful.

Another substantial number of people have experienced the second degree of thankfulness — being thankful in that one can give. You donate the clothes you haven't worn in the last two years or give some money to humanitarian organizations or volunteer your time to programs you believe in. There is that indescribable feeling that explains why people keep on giving of themselves and their resources.

When, however, you know someone (not a relative you may be obliged to help by cultural beliefs and/or practices) is thankful because of you, you are not only thankful because you can give but also in that someone else is thankful because you have touched his or her life and you know it at a personal level — that is a third degree of thankfulness, and only a few people experience it.

Like many readers of this story, I have been blessed in sharing my blessings through programs like YMCA, Women's and Children's Alliance, Rescue Mission, and American Red Cross. Doing so is a lifestyle that cannot be learned in college, and the "paycheck" is beyond anything corporate America can offer. Yet when your presence touches another human being on a one-on-one basis to a point that he or she is thankful, your thankfulness reaches another level.

The unique part of the whole experience is that you do not need to travel far from where you are to touch someone's life. Is there a senior citizen in your subdivision whom you can visit? Is there a child who does not live with one or both of his or her parents who can benefit from your presence and/or resources? Do you have a colleague who is going through family stress or illness and can use your shoulder to cry on?

There are no special skills needed for making another person have hope for a better tomorrow. There is no better time than doing it now when there is hope for improving their situation. The amazing aspect of your contribution is that you derive benefits beyond what the benefactor of your giving can fathom. Alex will never know what her thankfulness means to me.

CHAPTER 18

Give Your Best to Get the Best in Life

"Whatever you do for yourself can get you by. What you do for others is what gets you ahead; whether in your profession or personal or spiritual pursuits."

DR. VINCENT MULI WA KITUKU

A story is told of a farmer who gave the best of his seeds to his neighbors. He was also known to share his better breed bulls, in terms of fertility, during breeding seasons. This seemingly generous farmer provided educational opportunities for all the children in his village as well.

This farmer's way of life shocked one of his friends. "Why do you give your best seeds to your neighbors and even let them use your proven breeding bulls to breed their cows?" his bewildered friend asked. Before the farmer could respond, there was another question. "Don't you know these people are your competitors?"

After thinking about those questions the farmer responded, "They are not competitors. Yes, we sell our garden produce and dairy products at the same market. But that is not the whole picture. You see, when I give my best seeds to them, I am sure my crops will be cross-pollinated with the best. When I share my best bulls, I know there will always be the best within my village."

Even with this answer, his friend had one more thing to ask the farmer. "But why do you provide educational opportunities for their children when you could save your fortune for your own children and their families?"

Without mincing words, the farmer said, "I need workers who know what they are doing. Besides, when people are well educated, they have a chance of getting good jobs, and then you wouldn't have to worry about them stealing what you have. Because of this, I have never had the need to fence my property."

This story came to mind a few moments after I asked a colleague of mine to give me contacts for training material their office uses. The material was not developed exclusively for their office's needs. It was something available in the market, and I could have obtained the contacts elsewhere.

The cold response I got was, "I am not sure I should share this with you because you are our competitor." In over a decade of professional speaking, writing and consulting, this was the first and only time that I had come across this way of thinking.

The reason behind the success of the top performers in any chosen field can largely be attributed to the unrestrained giving of their wisdom, time and resources. They have mentored others. They have pointed to open doors for others to enter through the gates of opportunities. They have let would-be competitors learn what it takes to stay ahead. Masters of the craft have no worry in showing others "the ropes" of their jungle.

Stephen Covey reminds us that the best way to learn something is by teaching it to others. What we give is what we can keep for the rest of our lives. When we give our best, we get the best. The best way to have an advantage over your competitors is to have them talk nicely of your services and/or products. I do believe that God does bless those who bless others in ways the bottom line cannot measure.

CHAPTER 19

Springboard for Professional and Personal Growth

"Even if it's a little thing, do something for those who have a need of help, something for which you get no pay but the privilege of doing it."

DR. ALBERT SCHWEITZER, MEDICAL MISSIONARY AND NOBEL PEACE PRIZE WINNER

Serving others is a springboard that takes our whole realm of life to another level. When it happens, you remember it for the rest of your life. It is a moment when you feel like you have been given a new lease on your life. The cloud that has darkened your soul is lifted. You have a rekindled hope. You have a focused sense of who you are regardless of the prevailing circumstances. Your purpose in this world is renewed. You can't lay low any longer. You hold your head up one more time because there is a tomorrow to look forward to.

I was serving Thanksgiving dinner at the Boise Rescue Mission when one of the Idaho's elected officials happened to be there with his wife. The director of the men's program at Boise Rescue Mission showed me a copy of the Mission's book that I wrote a few years ago. In that book was a page with an old photo of this official serving food at the Mission.

During a short break, I showed him the photo. His whole body responded the way one reacts after meeting with a loved one that has disappeared and left no hope for his coming back.

With unreserved excitement, he called his wife, "Honey, come see this!"

As she was admiring his youthful appearance of years gone by, he said, "Vincent, thank you for showing me this photo. I came to serve food but left feeling like I had a moment of self-redemption."

Out of curiosity I asked him, "Why?"

What he said and how he said it left a mark in my heart. "Vincent, that moment occurred at the time I was going through a divorce and I had just been arrested for DUI."

His shining face explained what he didn't say in words.

As I drove home I recalled experiences of unexplained fulfillment even when not assured of the next meal as I left a prison where my mother had sent me to give some food to an incarcerated relative. That experience reappeared in high school when I helped raise money for youth activities or after teaching adults how to count from 1 to 10 or to say their ABCs.

Serving meals for the homeless or visiting a veteran or raking the yard for a senior citizen or doing anything that brings hope to youth is the cheapest and yet the most effective way of not only learning the joy of living but living your life to the fullest. A part of your life, time, or resources is sacrificed for another person's well-being.

Here are some things you will discover when you serve others:

1. Your faith starts having a new meaning as your perspective of life reaches new horizons.
2. You can never suffer from low self-esteem when serving someone in a worse condition than yours.
3. You experience an inward rejuvenation that an outward appearance can never substitute.
4. You don't have to be told what fulfillment means in life — you experience it.

5. Your desire to make your own life better becomes a natural thing.
6. Whatever challenges you are facing seem smaller when you compare them with what the folks you serve are experiencing.
7. You don't have to spend a penny to know the meaning of a rich life.
8. You don't have to worry about your worthiness.
9. The best gift you can ever give is your time.
10. You experience the fullness of life that comes when your gain outweighs what you give.
11. You learn that doing a good thing makes you want to do more.

The moment the official at the rescue mission experienced and other such moments in life are the oil that keeps you young and provide the wings you need to reach new heights of spiritual, personal and professional growth. Those moments cost you nothing more than your willingness to bring hope to a friend in need. And as strange as it sounds, you benefit in ways that tangible rewards can't pay for. You will know the meaning of a blessed life.

That official had served Thanksgiving dinners before. But when he did it at one of his darkest times of life, that act brought a new meaning to his life — again affirming that good deeds are rewarded.

CHAPTER 20

Be a Positive Outlier and Change Your World

An outlier is a character, not the average, that influences the outcome of a situation. The first outlier I witnessed was my father. This was before I was a graduate teaching assistant of statistics at the University of Wyoming, where I had in-depth lessons on how a single character or a small part of a large population can create havoc in studies.

Dad demanded the best of my brother and me. When he knew we would be late arriving to school in the morning, he went to the school office and asked the teacher on duty to cane us. If we were not among the top students, he did the spanking himself. For the record, he spanked me when I placed 6th in a class of 120 students.

He never bought us long trousers or shoes until we were admitted to government-aided high schools. His thinking was that such luxuries would distract us from the task at hand — preparing for a better future. He owned and operated a small clothing shop, selling the items we couldn't wear.

Our home, it seemed, was a test site for young people's ability to do manual chores. We worked hard, even during some public holidays. Dad believed you couldn't have the strength to attend the festivities that were part of the holidays on an empty stomach. So you had to earn your keep.

What Dad demanded was different. You must be different to make a difference. My uncle, cousins and my best friends had shoes and long trousers. They worked, but we worked harder.

We were, to the best of my knowledge, the only ones spanked for mediocre academic performance.

Dad was nicknamed Ian Smith, the last colonial ruler of what used to be Northern Rhodesia, because of what seemed to be his unreasonable expectations. Without details, I'll just say that only my brother and I, in that group of uncles, cousins and primary school friends, were admitted to the university after passing exams that terminated the futures of thousands.

Here are key aspects of a positive and effective outlier, if you are to influence people for success in any endeavor in life.

1. **You must be inspired by two passions: love and hate.** You must love the future you want to have regardless of what others say or do. You must also hate the status quo, mediocrity, and complacence.

2. **You must see things differently and act differently.** An outlier can never settle for what the average masses accept.

3. **You must inspire people to focus on their long term goal.** My father inspired us by promising to provide watches, suits and even cash if we were admitted to the university. When I achieved Upper Second Honors, he bought a new graduation gown for me. I kept it.

4. **You can never second guess your decisions and actions.** When your conscience is clear on the socio-economic benefits of your vision, don't second guess yourself.

5. **Learn to move forward.** Even when naysayers busy themselves with what they think you can't achieve, move forward.

6. **Keep rejuvenating your enthusiasm.** Learn new strategies to turn your goals into reality.

7. **Remove bitterness from your heart.** The best revenge is to do what your critics said you couldn't.

8. **Do not sit and hope things will change.** Outliers get up and create the change they envision.

When you think of it, George Washington was an outlier and so were characters such as Dr. Martin Luther King, Galileo, Mother Teresa, Joan of Arc, and Nelson Mandela.

Are you a positive outlier?

When an outlier is removed from a set of data, its influence is gone. In your sphere of life or work, would your absence be noticeable? Would people wish you were still available to affect their work or life in a positive way?

You don't need talent to be an outlier. You need a vision of the future you want, decisions to get you started on a path toward your vision and actions that bring you results.

CHAPTER 21

It Takes a Pack of Lions to Bring a Buffalo Down

If it takes a pack of four to five lions to bring a buffalo down, what makes you think you can overcome changes alone? You can only succeed in whatever you do, if you work with others!

Traditional knowledge has it that in some communities, when a buffalo was sighted, people would gather with spears and form a circle as they approached it. One person would spear the buffalo and then run away. As the buffalo pursued the first spear-thrower, another person speared it from another side. The buffalo would change direction and run toward the source of new pain. This went on until the beast was overpowered.

Are you using whatever "spear" you have to make your team successful? Here are key aspects to ponder.

1. Know the nature of your buffaloes. You can only address what you have identified.
2. What would happen if you didn't do anything to overcome your challenges?
3. Have a big picture. How is your life going to be different after you overcome your "buffaloes?"
4. Who else is fighting the same buffalo? That's your team.
5. Be adaptable. Teams change those who can't change for the team.
6. Learn to communicate effectively and all the time. Team success depends on many ideas channeled to achieve a single goal — overcoming buffaloes.

7. Be disciplined. This is the currency for accomplishing goals and winning championships.

8. Forget internal competition — be collaborative. Winning as a team is a byproduct of working together.

9. Develop unwavering commitment. Winning is not a matter of chance.

10. Enlarge your skills. Sharing your skills with teammates is your quickest way to grow your skills.

11. "One finger can't kill a louse." There is no I in the word TEAM. Be selfless.

12. Be conscious of your actions. Make every decision and action intentionally and with the purpose of contributing to success.

13. Plant in the dry season. Prepare before circumstances force you to.

14. You cannot cry your way to success. Your enthusiasm is the fuel for team success.

15. Be the go-to team player — the one the coach can call at any time for any play. Be dependable.

16. Learn to get along with teammates — if you will, they will.

17. Your team can never improve unless you are improving yourself.

18. Focus on solutions.

19. Take care of other issues that can distract you from your main goal.

20. Have deep-rooted hope even when there is no logical reason for it.

21. Never ever quit until you overcome your buffalo — until you accomplish your mission.

CHAPTER 22

Overcoming Buffaloes in an Unpredictable Workplace

Call it offshore sourcing, but what you have witnessed is jobs made obsolete by the bad economy, declining product prices, war uncertainty, and competition with international businesses that are subsidized by their governments.

It seems that neither employers nor employees can any longer accurately anticipate these changes before they occur. Such unexpected changes could be compared to the appearance of water buffaloes in an African village. Buffaloes invaded villages without warning, devastating social structures, uprooting the harmonious livelihood of villagers and leaving them feeling insecure and stressed out.

This is a confounding situation — bad for employers because employees' optimal performance requires a secure job environment, and stress-related illnesses may lead to increased absenteeism. Employees, on the other hand, need great performance to be marketable and keep their organization profitable.

What can be done to overcome these "social buffaloes" in the workplace? Organizations, private or public, won't revert to the old womb-to-tomb job security. Job availability and longevity will continue to be dictated by factors beyond the control of workers and even employers. The resumé that got you where you are probably won't keep you there beyond the foreseeable future.

Yet, we should never underestimate the fact that change presents opportunities for tapping into one's often hidden potential and creativity. The question is:

How do you motivate yourself, feel secure, stress less and thrive in these chaotic times?

1. **Become multi-functional.** What did you do in the past that you can revert to if your position is no longer available? What are the skills, knowledge and abilities that you are using now that you can transfer to another employer if need be? Use your talents and skills as if you own the organization. After every six months, your resumé should have new lines of quantifiable and profitable project(s) you have accomplished.

2. **Assume nothing.** Your job, employer and work location can change. Flexibility must become a necessary survival tool. Remember the down-to-earth wisdom, "Blessed are the flexible, for they shall never be bent out of shape."

3. **Use network and teamwork skills.** Master the elements of team-building and success. These include commitment, interpersonal communication skills, unselfish contributions, coordination, conflict and change management, and a willingness to learn from diverse cultural and professional backgrounds. Volunteering in community services is a great way to learn, contribute and make your talents and interests known. The intangible rewards are invaluable.

4. **Stay in school.** Helen Hayes said, "When books are opened, we discover our wings." Your vehicle's CD/cassette player is a mobile college at your fingertips. Keep yourself marketable by continuously improving your skills, knowledge and abilities. In the jungle, whether you are a lion or gazelle, when the sun is up, you'd better be running for survival.

5. **Remember, a job alone cannot provide long-term security.** There must be a balancing and blending of one's relationships, recreation, and personal and professional growth. Cleave to aspects of life money can't pay for.

CHAPTER 23

The Perfect Way to Lose
Playing for Individual Glory
in a Team Project

My team's downfall was a direct result of a successful soccer season — we won all the games before the tournaments. Did I do something wrong?

It takes an individual to score some points but it takes a team to win a game. Yet this is not just a sports issue. As a leader, you know the productivity of your organization can be way below expectations, even though you have experienced and talented employees, just because one or a few individuals don't see the process as a team activity. Even churches have been brought down by individuals with personal goals.

Lack of a 100 percent commitment to a team effort but a 100 percent commitment to individual glory is the best way to have an overall mediocre team performance. Each team member has to devote 100 percent effort to the group's goal, even at the expense of personal gratification.

In my fourth season as a youth soccer coach, I designed a strategy that seemed like a miracle answer to our previous heartbreaking season. We had lost all but two games in our third season. My strategy — let each player experience the thrill of being a winner. Every single player had scored a goal by the end of the fourth game of the season.

The weekly game plan was simple — get the top players to defend our goal and let the best shooters score (in a commanding way) in the first quarter. Then move other players to the frontline and let the strikers pass the ball to them. It was one of those moments that time cannot erase from a coach's mind. To see a nine-year-old boy score his first goal ever and then take a victory run toward his parents, who were in disbelief, was unforgettable. I saw it happen week after week until the players with the least scores had each made four goals.

Unknown to me, that thrill had become something each player wanted to experience in each game by the end of the regular season. Will, one of the kids you just had to love for his free spirit, was the first to show this hidden agenda. I assigned him to a position in the back of the field but he let me know that he wanted to go to a striker's position so that he could score "his goal." That was not a problem since we had secured a spot for the tournaments.

At the first game of the tournament, the team we played against scored first, and I noticed my goal-keeper, one of the top players (fast, confident and loved the sport) crying. He was not crying because of the goal just scored against his team. He was crying because as a goal-keeper he could not score a goal.

You may have seen major outstanding teams lose games they could have won mainly because individual players focused more on what they could achieve instead of their team's overall success.

Individuals can score points but it takes a team effort to win games.

A team's success makes individual performance stand out.

CHAPTER 24

Become a Maximum Impact Player
What Assets to Possess and Develop

*"We are what we repeatedly do. Excellence, then,
is not an act, but a habit."*

ARISTOTLE

Are you a maximum impact player?

Do you perform at a level that makes your chances of failing a non-issue?

In whatever endeavor we choose to pursue in life, there are a few qualities we can master to increase our chances of success — qualities that we can depend on in critical moments when our future is on the brink of being determined by the outcome of whatever we are doing.

With the game tied 42-42 and 1:11 to play, the San Jose Spartans needed a 30-yard field goal to beat the nationally ranked Boise State Broncos. The stakes were high for the Broncos. Boise was to no longer be the team with the most consecutive wins (20 at the time) nationally. The team had not lost in 14 nationally televised games. Chances of the Broncos being invited to a respectable bowl game would be thwarted by losing to a team ranked among the least, not only in the Western Athletic Conference, but also at the national level.

The past glory was well established, but their bright future was at a critical moment. You can imagine the weight and the degree of intensity as the Broncos prepared their special team for the greatest mission at that moment. Their mission: block the field goal.

Each of the team's players ran to their positions, and the Spartan's field goal kicker tapped his kicking leg while he waited for the ball to be in place. When the play was on, the ball was passed to the holder who placed it in position for the kicker. In a split second, in that defining moment, the Boise State Broncos did what needed to be done — block the ball. The Broncos had put in position two of their top jumpers.

The game went on to two overtimes before the Broncos outlasted the Spartans with a 56-49 win. This was the fifth time in the season that the Broncos had displayed qualities of maximum impact players.

Meeting with Dan Hawkins, head coach of Boise State University football team, a week after that game, I asked him what it takes to be in a special team. I explained that I would like to teach the concept that we can achieve maximum results in whatever we do, as I had seen his players do time and again.

The response somehow surprised me. Mr. Hawkins didn't mention talent as the main quality. Instead, he said that *the key is to have people who understand the importance of what you want to accomplish, especially in that critical moment* — people who understand the big picture, then focus on the task at hand, and do it with maximum effort for maximum impact. You want people who are consistent.

So first come qualities that can be developed. "And of course talent helps," Dan said.

This affirmed my long-held conviction that hard work, when concentrated on an expected outcome, will beat talent when talent takes things for granted.

Think about being in a special team at your work. You don't necessarily need special talents. Understand what needs to be achieved. Understand how what you do contributes to the big picture. Be willing to go the extra mile and give of yourself for the success of the team. Do this whenever you have the opportunity.

In closing, Dan Hawkins shared with me that after the starting players are identified for out-of-town games, a coach next picks players who can play in special teams.

Uncertainties abound in the workplace as jobs keep going overseas and non-stop organizational restructurings lead to layoffs in the thousands. It's therefore of paramount importance to have what it takes to perform for maximum impact and to be kept in the "special team squad."

CHAPTER 25

Focus: A Lesson Learned From Steers

When I was growing up in Kenya, we prepared our land for planting during the dry season. The soil was hard to cultivate by hand, so we used draft animals. With yoked steers, we were able to plow large areas in a short time.

When I had the steers harnessed, I called my younger brother to direct the steers as I plowed. I had to put pressure on the plough in order to turn the soil thoroughly and remove weeds.

The smoothness with which the steers pulled the plow depended on the direction they were going, toward home or away from home. When they pulled toward home, it seemed like they moved in a straight line. My brother didn't need to put pressure on them. When they were pulled away from home, they moved in a crooked manner, and pressure had to be applied to make them cut a straight line.

The hardness of the soil was the same, but the direction the steers were pulling made the difference. Their focus was HOME. That was their goal.

Focus is the driving force that galvanizes all aspects needed to achieve an established goal at a given time with limited resources.

The force that significantly impacts the productivity of individuals and organizations is based on why and where they set their **focus**, how they set it and when they set it.

We focus on what is beneficial to us. If it improves our finances, relationships, beauty or skills, then we channel our energy toward it. Focus can be either on the past or future, obstacles or opportunities.

Focusing on the past or negative experience is the best way to waste energy and resources.

Problems with focusing on obstacles or bad experiences from the past:
- Wastes time blaming others.
- Destroys creativity.
- Develops defensiveness.
- Illuminates what's wrong rather than what's right.
- Wastes energy and resources.
- Keeps people stuck in their mindset.
- Creates environment for negative feedback as more problems are caused by focused attention on old problems.
- Leads to business failure, broken relationships, fumbled careers and regret.

Focusing on opportunities and future needs dictates how resources are utilized for maximum results.

Benefits of focusing on opportunities and solutions:
- Makes obstacles seem smaller.
- Creates an environment for creativity and enthusiasm.
- Illuminates what's working and/or what can work in the future.
- Propels people toward their goals.
- Involves others.
- Leads to strong relationships, business success, and hope.

CHAPTER 28

You Must Always Have Unfinished Business

"It's what you know after you know it all that counts."
JOHN WOODEN

Yesterday, he was on top of his game. Today, it seems he is nowhere near his best. The fastest way for an achiever to revert to mediocrity in any calling or profession is to have no unfinished business. Competitive edge, continuous growth and success are loosely tied to achieving established goals. The key is to turn yesterday's goals into today's routine. Then make it the platform you need to set goals that are more challenging, the ones you didn't think of yesterday. You must see and set yourself up for a life beyond today's goals.

Why people succeed and then don't remain successful is a phenomenon that has crossed my mind since my days of youth in Kangundo, Kenya, as I painfully witnessed talented and successful students fail in exams after spectacular performance in previous testing.

To be admitted to government high school during my days, seventh grade students had to complete three exams: mathematics, English and general paper (this included geography, history, civics and general sciences). In the year I passed (I had failed in the previous year), only about 10 students in a class of 120 received passing grades on the high school admission exam.

My high school class had 120 students who were there on academic merits. After four years only about 15 students passed another exam to qualify for the final two years of high school. Out of the 15 talented students, three of us went to university after passing an exam that forced our classmates to be left behind.

There are many parameters one can examine to determine what happened to the otherwise brilliant after being successful. Adjustments to living away from our parents, the freedom of making decisions about one's life, or the subjects we studied are some factors that might have affected how these students thrived. Some students didn't have time to study because they were preoccupied with family matters.

Yet that is what you see with teams, businesses, and individuals that were once a success story. You see the efforts, the focus, the exceptional customer service and the attention paid to details that helped them climb to the top. You see the fruits when the team, business or an individual is at the top. Then you see that yesterday's success disappears into the unknown with unbelievable speed. You are then left with one question, "What went wrong?"

A team, business or an individual without unfinished business is a finished business — until some serious rethinking, refocusing and redetermining of what brought success and how to stay successful is done and then followed by action.

1. **Loss of the initial vision, focus and determination.** Think of the vision you had. How focused were you when you began? Is your determination the same?

2. **Relishing the success of the moment for too long.** In my school, this was sad. Some of my fellow students relished their flying colors in past exams, but took no time to focus and prepare for what was ahead.

3. **Not adjusting soon enough for the challenges of new circumstances.** Today's world is different from that of our parents, whether in workplaces or at home. You have to evaluate where you are and what you must do to stay on top and adapt to the new challenges.

4. **Assuming that what got you there will keep you there.** This is the fastest way to fall back faster than you climbed up. Competitors are also "climbing." New methods of doing things are constantly being developed. Be in tune with what's new.

5. **Having pride, arrogance and an I-know-it-all attitude.** I rest my case. But I must share one observation. It seemed like joining high school made some students forget that they still belonged to the Kamba tribe. Some came home, after just three months in a boarding school, pronouncing Kamba words with the same accent as European missionaries. Their walking style and their manners, too, had changed. It was hard to watch these students humbled back to the Kamba way of life by the next exam — when they failed.

6. **Forgetting that you have to keep growing to stay on top.** When you don't grow, you go.

7. **Inability to develop a new vision.** A vision creates new challenges to overcome, new territories to conquer, and new heights to attain.

You know where you are. You know how you got there. You know what is not working. How can you "pass" the next exam?

CHAPTER 27

Turn Setbacks into Opportunities For a Better Future

"Things turn out the best for those who make the best of the way things turn out."

JOHN WOODEN

A story is told of how an old donkey turned misfortune into opportunity. The donkey had given its owner, a farmer, service for many years. When it was too old to do anything, the farmer thought of putting it to permanent sleep, but he was not ready emotionally.

However, as the donkey was grazing it fell into a pit. The farmer thought, "Oh, well, since the donkey is just waiting for death, I will just cover it with soil instead of trying to help it out of the pit." He shoveled soil into the pit. When the donkey felt something strange on its back, he shook his body and the soil fell off. The farmer continued shoveling soil and the donkey continued shaking it off its back. Soon the donkey, stepping on the soil that was supposed to bury it, got from the pit and lived its full life.

In life, setbacks are sometimes the best steppingstones for a new beginning.

One sure thing in life is that no one is exempt from life's setbacks. As you read this piece, the material to "bury" you may be divorce, being laid off, illness, betrayal, or the death of a loved one. Your children may be dancing to a different drum beat or making wrong choices.

Your ability to bounce back starts the moment you accept your vulnerability, admit any fear or anxiety and become willing to endure and fully experience your pain and suffering.

- Reflect on the highlights of your situation, lessons learned and how they can be useful later on.
- Find the parts of your situation you can manage easily.
- Share your setbacks and their implication in your life.
- Learn to take less responsibility so you can have time to yourself and avoid being burdened.
- Turn resentment into forgiveness.
- Forgive yourself and those you might blame for your failure or loss.
- Don't give loneliness a chance. Network with others and attend social events.
- Seek the meaning of your crisis in terms of your spiritual, social and professional aspects.

Ask yourself, "From here, now where?"

What can you do to better your life and the lives of those who have suffered the same loss?

One effective way of turning your setbacks into steppingstones is by helping others who might suffer from similar setbacks.

CHAPTER 28

Let Your Chair Remain Where It Belongs — in the Past

"My contemplation of life...taught me that he who cannot change the very fabric of his thought...will never be able to change reality, and will never, therefore, make any progress."

ANWAR SADAT, LATE PRESIDENT OF EGYPT

Did you know that many people would lead better lives if only they could let the past remain where it belongs — in the past? Did you know that past failing experiences, disappointments, or fumbled dreams and relationships, if focused on, have the ability to not only limit one's potential for fulfillment but can also destroy creativity, the ability to develop new relationships, and chances for work and life balance?

In my presentations, I have used a chair to demonstrate how past detrimental experiences can be the main obstacle to the future or present life of fulfillment you want. You stand up from your chair to go to the door. However, before you take a step you pick up the chair and place it in front of your path. That chair becomes the obstacle between you and the door.

Millions of people in the workplace and other settings of life have limited their opportunities for growth because they are too attached to a past of mediocre performance, past negative criticisms, or simply past failing experiences. After ten years of working with hundreds of thousands of people from all walks of life and from all continents, I have been overwhelmed by inspirational stories of people who have overcome devastating pasts. Some are so drastic that it sounds like you are listening to the narration of a fiction movie.

Yet, others stories are disheartening. Those are stories where an individual's present and future hope, vision, and goals are blurred by a past they can't change.

Thinking about this brings to mind a story I read. It was about two monks who vowed never to talk to a woman. As they were traveling they found a young girl who couldn't walk, stranded. One monk had pity on that girl and carried her to her home that was along their path.

A few hours later, he realized that his friend had not talked to him and asked him why he was silent. The friend answered and said, "You messed up our vows when you carried that girl." That is when the merciful monk said, "I am sorry you are still carrying that girl. I left her five hours ago."

Are you still carrying your past? Here are some key ways to leave your messed up past behind.

1. **Exercise forgiveness.** It takes a strong person to forgive himself and others for past hurts. You liberate your energy and creativity and focus better when you forgive parents, teachers, bosses, colleagues or those mean people who purposely hurt you. When you forgive, you give yourself the opportunity to live a new rewarding life.

2. **Create a new vision.** There must be a present and a future that is different from the past you dislike. It's hard to leave a past and enter an unknown present or future. What attributes

of life, that are different from your past, would you like to experience?

3. **Develop new relationships.** One element that keeps people in a circle of disappointments is the company they maintain. Bring achievers into your life and your life will be a life of achieving.

4. **Get involved in wholeness activities.** Find programs that provide you with the opportunity to grow spiritually, mentally and physically on a daily basis. These aspects of life are the foundation from which you begin to create the world of your dreams.

5. **Develop other people.** There is probably no better way to turn your painful past into something of beauty than to help those who are traveling the same path you traveled or help prevent others from experiencing your dreadful errors.

Remember, you have the ability to start living the life of your dreams now, so long as you are willing to leave your "chairs" where they belong — in the past.

CHAPTER 29

The Big Picture

"The worth of a life is not determined by a single failure or a solitary success."

KEVIN KLINE, ACTOR

One way ecologists study tree age and forest fire patterns is by looking at cross sections of trees that have lived many years. Each ring represents a year of growth. The rings of the trees are usually easily seen, but some show up more than others.

Some rings are particularly dark, suggesting that there were forest fires in those years, and the growth of the tree was affected. Other rings may be thinner than the rest because drastic conditions impaired normal growth. However, based on the tree's general appearance, those darker or thinner rings may be only minor discoloration on a mass of healthy and ordinary rings.

From this natural school, we learn that it is the big picture of life that is important, not our drawbacks.

How is your big picture?

Do you focus on the "minor discoloration" that might have happened in the past?

Even in those times when the tree is "tried by fire," some kind of growth occurred. Likewise, our drawbacks may present opportunities for us to grow, albeit probably not as much as in normal circumstances.

Past "darker or thinner" parts of our lives may leave physical or emotional marks that may cause difficulty in focusing on the big picture of life. The normal and healthy rings reflect the fact that a tree utilizes available resources maximally in good seasons. Two resources, you and time, are crucial and must be utilized wisely. You shouldn't spend your time reminiscing on wounds of the past. Doing so only steals from your current and future resources. It is chasing the wind.

No matter how dark your past professional and personal life has been, your future, which starts now, is unmarred. Henry Miller said, *"What seems nasty, painful, evil can become a source of beauty, joy and strength, if faced with an open mind. Every moment is a golden one for him who has the vision to recognize it as such."*

CHAPTER 30

The Best Gift: Having Daddy Home

"Other things may change us, but we start and end with family."

ANTHONY BRANDT

Whenever my father went to Nairobi, Kenya, from our village, chances were that he would bring something for our mother and sometimes for us, his children. The gifts for children could be candies or a shirt or shorts. I always looked forward to his coming, hoping that there would be something for me.

I started my own family in the early 1980s and adopted my father's habit. Whenever I was away for one or two nights, I would make sure I had something for my wife and children. Sometimes my schedule made it hard for me to get time for shopping for gifts. In such situations, I would arrange with my wife for time to shop on our way home after she picked me up from the airport, just to buy gifts for the children.

Well, that was before I became a full-time speaker and business trainer. Most of my schedules in the last few years don't allow me time to shop. Thus, with time my father's habit has unintentionally been left behind.

But when Celina, my daughter, was eight years old she brought me to tears as she and her two older sisters were discussing the gifts I used to bring home. They talked about how they used to wait in anticipation for the gifts and also noted they now didn't get those gifts so often.

At this point Celina hugged me and said, "Oh, well, the best gift is to have Daddy home." Bless her heart!

Again, there is no substitute for a father in a child's life unless the absence is due to natural causes. A loving father's presence and involvement in a child's life provides emotional security that helps the child to develop the wings he or she needs to soar in an uncertain world.

As a father I have found some trivial things I do with my children that are monumental in their lives.

Here are some:

- Take each child alone for lunch.
- Let your child hear you cancel a business appointment because you have just realized he or she has an event you want to attend.
- Visit his or her class (I go tell African folktales and show slides of where I grew up – this is a hit program).
- Read to them.
- Share your stories.
- Have your child retell the stories he or she learned in school.
- Share funny cartoons or e-mail messages with your child.
- Read a book your child is reading in school, and discuss it.
- Recognize your child for something he or she didn't think was important.
- Write a thank you note to your child's teacher or call and tell him or her how much you appreciate the positive influence the teacher has on your child's life.
- Take the family out or do something as a family in honor of your child's achievement, no matter how mundane.
- Know the name and something about his or her best friend.

Regardless of culture, religion or social status, a child's strong relationship with his/her father reduces chances of rebellion. In addition to being a father, being your child's friend opens up doors of opportunities to learn his or her world. Today's children's world is different from ours. Still remember: "Oh, well, the best gift is to have Daddy home."

CHAPTER 31

The Mistake of Overworking

This career woman had been going to work earlier than anyone else. She worked through her lunch hours and stayed late after everyone had left the office. She took work home. It was this way until one day, her four-year-old daughter picked up the file of work her mom had brought and tossed it across the room. When mom asked why she threw the papers, the youngster said, "I hate your work."

I wish I could say I made up this story to make a point. But it is an incident that happened. Work had robbed a young girl time with her mother. At four, she showed her frustration in the best way she knew how. The incident brought back a bitter memory of my own rude awakening.

My daughter's teacher had asked me to come to the school to tell African folktales. After my presentation, my child hugged me and said, "Dad, thank you for coming. See you tomorrow morning." The surprised teacher asked her, "Is your dad not coming home tonight? Why did you say, 'see you tomorrow?'" My child, in second grade at the time, innocently said, "My dad works until late at night. He comes home when I am already asleep. I only see him in the morning as he prepares to leave."

It's sad that we operate at breakneck pace. There are those who don't even take vacations they have earned — no time to spend with family. Vacation locations are filled with vacationers hooked to their cell phones or laptops. I just witnessed a man doing his job's paperwork at a restaurant while his wife quietly sat watching guests as they came and left.

Jobs may bring precious gems. But relationships are priceless. No tangible value can be attached to the experience of playing a game with your children, watching them score in a game or reading together. No price can be attached to the time a couple spends together.

Wise leaders today are not looking for people who put in long hours. They want people with a balanced life; people with non-work related priorities that they have the same enthusiasm for as they have for their jobs. They want double hitters — people who work hard and play hard.

There is danger in letting our jobs come to be closer to our hearts than our families. Jobs come and go. Positions we hold in public service are also for a relatively short time. Family ties are forever (or should be) — the thread that lasts long after who we worked for, what we did, and how much we made are long forgotten.

CHAPTER 32

A Few Days in My Wife's Shoes

I could not understand why my father was giving his in-laws the one cow that provided milk for our family. Through family discussions, I had learned that my father's family had given my mother's family more than the traditional token of appreciation, commonly known in the West as dowry.

Since my younger brother and I were the ones asked to deliver the cow to my maternal grandparents, I asked Dad why; a 17-year-old son needed an explanation for the meaning of this transfer. Dad said that when a man is blessed with a good wife, he has to show his in-laws his appreciation from time to time. He mentioned that there was no price for a good wife and the gifts given to in-laws was a continuous way of saying thank you.

Of course, the tradition of dowry has been misunderstood and misused, especially by those less attached to its significance.

But it is the value of a good wife that has kept my mind thinking of my father's words. I have nursed the knowledge that I been outrageously blessed with a marvelous wife for over twenty years. That said, the challenge of being in my wife's shoes for few days was humbling and revealing.

For months I knew she would attend a conference for a lengthy period of time — four days. That meant my being home with two of our three daughters (13 and 10) and son (6). I kept the thoughts of her being absent in the back of my mind until I realized I could not ignore the fact that I was afraid of being home alone.

A week before she left for the conference, she had to leave early in the morning for a meeting. By default I was in charge of getting the children ready for school. One of them was sick and I had to call my wife to ask which medicine I was to give her. By the time I had found it, the sick child and her brother had rushed to the bus. I rushed to the bus, too, not only with medicine but also with another form that needed a parent's signature but had slipped my attention. The gracious bus driver just laughed when I said "This is Parenting 101" as I gave medicine to my daughter and signed the form.

At dinner time that evening, as I bragged about my effectiveness that morning, my daughter told me that I gave her nighttime medicine. Further, my son let me know that the form I labored to sign had been due a month earlier. Oh my! I induced my daughter to sleep in class. And my son had a worthless form signed by me.

Two days before my wife's departure, my daughters surprised me with how concerned they were at having dad as their cook. The 13-year-old said, "I know what we are going to eat until Mom comes.

"Ugali on the first day, followed by Ugali every night."

Ugali, corn meal, is the main food where I grew up.

Without hesitation, her 10-year-old sister looked at me with appealing eyes and said, "I know Dad won't torture us that way. He will get us a pizza." My wife laughed so hard I had to join.

On the day my beloved left, I had to pray for my children while I was still in bed before they left for school — they had prepared themselves. I had not slept the previous night, since I spent it preparing myself mentally to be home alone with children scared of my cooking.

The after school activities were the next test of my parenthood.

Knowing that the 13-year-old had a basketball game, I had to pick up the other two from their school and head to the game. Out of my heart's goodness, I decided to carry snacks.

The way they found the snacks and started eating them forced me to ask, "Does Mom bring you snacks to eat before you go to the game?"

And the answer was a definitive "YEAH."

One day with my wife away from home felt like a decade of crisis. My professional creativity and performance recoiled to levels I am ashamed of. What mothers do can only be understood by being in their shoes.

Now I understand why Dad found fulfillment in giving his in-laws the cow that was invaluable. It was a token of his appreciation for the invaluable child (my mother) they had blessed him with. God bless wives.

CHAPTER 33

What Would You Hold If Mt. Vesuvius Erupted in Your Backyard?

The ancient city of Pompeii lies at the foot of Mt. Vesuvius in Italy. For years Pompeii was a flourishing port and a prosperous trading city. However, in 79 AD, an eruption of Mt. Vesuvius buried Pompeii under cinders and ashes that preserved its ruins. According to a story I heard from Glenna Salsbury at the 1997-98 President of National Speakers Association, most of the 20,000 dwellers escaped, but about 2,000 were left behind and perished.

The ruins of Pompeii were discovered in 1748 and archeological excavations have revealed the habits and cultural practices of the dwellers. Some of those who perished were grasping personal or family treasures. A man's skeleton was found clutching a beautiful bronze statue. A woman's skeleton held a bunch of jewels, and a couple held a wooden box filled with treasures.

This scenario comes to mind every time I get an unexpected mail, fax or e-mail on how to be successful. The messages emphasize how much money to make, where to go for vacation, what kind of house and neighborhood to live in, what model of car to drive or what treasure to buy for loved ones. These things are measures of success in our times.

Our generation did not initiate material possessions as a measure of success. However, in many cultures, success had another angle: happiness in one's life and in the lives of those held dear. These cultures, while stripped of modern measures of success, have intact and thriving relationships. Family ties are their social security, and the well-being of the youth is their assurance for a bright future.

Material possessions do make life easier, but they cannot provide inner peace. One's search for the meaning of life, fulfillment, identity and worth cannot be achieved through possessions. Ponder this: Money can buy a bed, but it can't make you fall asleep in that bed. It can buy the best food, but not the appetite to enjoy the food. Money can buy a house, but not a peaceful and happy home. It can buy medicine, but not healing. Money may provide the means of prolonging life, but its purse can do nothing to assure eternal life.

Loving relationships are what matters. That's the glue of life. It is love that develops from the basics of life and is not based on the artificiality of material gain.

The story of Pompeii brings back memories of my loved ones who have passed on. I know that what my heart cherishes most is the quality times we spent together. Memories of cherished relationships are treasures that lighten the hearts of our loved ones, when our lives are petrified in life's catastrophes like the eruption of Mt. Vesuvius. If Mt. Vesuvius were to erupt in our backyard today, what would we hold onto as a demonstration of our hearts' treasures?

CHAPTER 34

Balancing Work and Life

"There is nothing we can do that will bring us more in the way of rewards than daily striving to become better adjusted, happier, more productive human beings. It's a lifetime job and worth every minute we spend on it."

EARL NIGHTINGALE

Lee Iacocca, former chairman of Chrysler Corporation, said that most of the 242 million working people, "swing out of bed, yawn, and figure: 'Oh hell, I've got to make it through another day of drudgery.'" Working people are stressed out. Jack Canfield, author of Chicken Soup for the Soul, said that about 75 percent of workers don't like what they are doing or who they work for.

A major explanation for stress has been uncertainty in the workplace as a result of increased competition, changing local and international trade regulations, merging of corporations and technological advances. These changes have been experienced nationally and locally.

Is change new to humanity?

Are there better ways for an individual to thrive in a world of uncertainty?

How can one balance the demands of personal life and work?

To answer these questions, I am inclined to share strategies that were used by the people of my native community, Kamba, in Kenya. Their stresses were caused by disease, famine, the presence of buffaloes and unpredictable tribal wars. The stresses experienced by Kambas and those in today's workplace are similar because in both, one's security is threatened, there is a sense of loss of one's identity, and loyalty to a system is negatively affected.

Using the strategies of the Kambas can help balance work and personal life:

1. Individuals established their purpose on earth from a perspective that was independent from one's daily activities. In today's chaotic workplace, each one should ask himself:
   What is the primary purpose or mission in life?
   What is there to look back to and be glad of?

2. With the purpose established, an individual committed his vision, decisions and actions on activities that helped him achieve his purpose. He aligned individual goals with those of the group he belonged to.
   In what ways can your employment help you attain that purpose? How are your life goals aligning with the vision and mission of the organization you are working for?

3. Self empowerment allowed individuals to take risks and venture into unsettled lands with confidence. Working people have to develop self-empowering strategies that allow them to use their creative and authentic potential to achieve their purposes while they create an environment for their employer's success.

4. Natural and manmade changes were viewed as natural processes that perpetuated personal and community growth and new ways of survival. One has to view change in the workplace with an attitude of looking for new opportunities,

including chances to improve skills, knowledge and abilities, thus improving one's employability.

5. Individuals and the community had rituals that helped people bounce back after going through a devastating experience. Adherence to faith, reflection on what had happened, staying in contact with others and physical activities were springboards for the soul, body and mind as one forged ahead with his journey of accomplishing his mission. These are aspects that can be used by all of us to refocus our purpose during and after change.

6. Flexibility was a major survival strategy. People relocated or alternated livelihood from crop cultivators to livestock keepers to gatherers to hunters, based on prevailing conditions. The ability to let go of perceptions and practices that may not be beneficial to oneself or an organization is a stress-reduction step. "Utility players" (those who play different positions of a game) are always searched for. It has been said that, "Blessed are the flexible, for they shall not be bent out of shape."

7. Involvement in community affairs provided opportunities to learn, socialize, help others and strengthen a sense of belonging and contribution. Getting involved in one's community is not only a networking strategy, but an opportunity to help others, which is one of the secrets of success.

When work and personal life are balanced, good health, increased productivity, and fulfillment are realized.

Human Hair in My Chicken Meal
A Blessing in Disguise

"You cannot tailor-make the situations in life, but you can tailor-make the attitudes to fit those situations."

ZIG ZIGLAR

Your attitude toward everything in life will determine your peace of mind and both your short and long term success.

In the fall of 1986, God blessed me with a situation that should have been a depressing experience. I found a human hair in my food. It was a blessing in disguise. I had been in the United States for less than a year when I asked a friend of mine to take me to Denver, Colorado, to look for a car for my family. We shopped way past lunchtime and about 3:00 p.m., we decided to take a break to find a restaurant. My friend took me to a place where chicken meals were sold. The good smell and the appetizing look of the food were beyond my imagination.

Chicken in Kenya, where I grew up, was very expensive and many people could hardly afford it. Now, here I was at a well-known fried chicken restaurant. I enjoyed every bite with an intensity words cannot describe. But before I cleared my plate, I noticed a person's hair. I just wanted to put the hair aside and continue with my lunch. However, my friend saw it and immediately asked for the manager and showed him the hair in my almost finished food. The manager was so apologetic, but I couldn't understand what the big deal was.

Then the manager said the most heartwarming words of the day, "I will give you another plate of food. We are sorry for the hair."

I was not sorry for the hair. I was thankful for it. (Now I wonder how many other times I visited a chicken restaurant and looked for another hair just to be blessed with an extra plate of chicken.)

On reflection, I have thought of the many situations where we focus on trivial inconveniences and overlook the blessings that might be disguised. We complain about a rainy day at the expense of being thankful for the food that will be harvested, as a result of the rain, for our survival. We complain about our jobs instead of being thankful for our employment, especially in these times of massive downsizing. We complain about what we don't have instead of appreciating what we do have.

Having an attitude of gratitude is a choice we make as individuals. You can choose to see the "social hairs" in your life or the extra plates of blessings you get because of the hairs. Think of the clean water or the fact you may not have to worry about your next meal or your family or your health. And don't forget that if you are reading this book, you have been blessed with another day that many people didn't live to see.

Afterword

"Ula ukunyeewa niwe withuaa."

AKAMBA PROVERB

"He whose body is itching scratches himself."

Don't wait for others to formulate your success path. It's your life, family, career and soul; you are responsible for your life.

TAKEN FROM THE SCHOOL WITH NO WALLS WHERE LIFELONG LESSONS BEGIN BY DR. VINCENT MULI WA KITUKU

To grow, own what you do, and set yourself apart

1. Become a lifelong learner.
2. Be self-initiating.
3. Forget job descriptions; do what needs to be done.
4. Learn to look, ask and listen.
5. Always have something to live up to.
6. Take time to nurture your soul, body and mind.
7. Tap the richness of other people as a contributor and team player.
8. Learn to turn obstacles into opportunities.
9. Plant seeds for your professional and personal future growth NOW.

About the author

Dr. Vincent Muli Wa Kituku, a native of Kenya, works with organizations and individuals who want to increase their productivity, stay focused and have a sustained desire to make success a lifestyle and a choice. An international speaker, Dr. Kituku has given presentations for Fortune 500 companies and public organizations. A widely read, influential writer in business, inspiration and education, he has been described as a research-based motivational speaker/trainer whose storytelling skills have won awards for both spoken and written words.

Vincent is one of fewer than 7 percent of speakers who have earned the coveted Certified Speaking Professional (CSP) recognition, the highest designation presented by the National Speakers Association. He has been the motivational speaker for the successful Boise State University football team since 1998.

What is unparalleled, however, is Vincent's story of triumph over adversities. He refused to be held back or live a life defined by the deaths of five siblings, chronic malaria and stomach illnesses, spending six years in three grades or growing up in a dysfunctional family. With his signature positive attitude, big dreams and hard work, Vincent knew he would be somebody someday. These losses and setbacks made Dr. Kituku believe that each individual has the potential to soar to great heights if only they knew how.

Dr. Kituku received his Bachelor of Science degree from the University of Nairobi and both his Masters and Doctorate from the University of Wyoming. Vincent lives in Idaho with his wife and their four children.

OvercomingBuffaloes.com

At www.overcomingbuffaloes.com you can learn more about what Overcoming Buffaloes Keynotes and Seminars can provide for leaders and employees of your organization.

Have Dr. Vincent Muli Wa Kituku speak to your group. He brings passion people need to overcome their buffaloes. People from all backgrounds agree that words cannot describe Vincent—he must be experienced. His ability to captivate audiences with content, interaction and entertainment leaves them motivated, owning what they do, focused and ready to increase productivity. He is a dynamic keynote speaker.

Overcoming Buffaloes is dedicated to working with you and your organization to increase productivity through employee and leadership programs.

Join the Overcoming Buffaloes family. Sign up for the free monthly electronic newsletter at www.overcomingbuffaloes.com or contact us at:

Kituku & Associates
P.O. Box 7152
Boise, Idaho 83707
(888) 685-1621
(208) 376-8724

Additional Resources

Dr. Kituku's current and forthcoming recommended resources for professional and personal growth:

- Overcoming Buffaloes as a Leader
- Inspiring Productivity With Stories/Metaphors
- Overcoming Buffaloes in Marriages
- Overcoming Buffaloes Series with audio CD:
  9 Must Know Lessons for Being the CEO of All You Do, and 7 Actions That Make Failing a Non-option
- Outstanding Presentations: How to Put Your Presence in Your Presentations
- How to Speak and Get Paid
- Rays & Storms as the River Flows
- Mbathi Sya Kumutaia Mwiai (Gospel Songs in Kikamba)
- I Stopped Raising Angels to Raise Children With Human Characteristics
- The School With No Walls
- Multicultural Folktales for All Ages
- East African Folktales for All Ages
- The Voice of Mukamba: African Motivational Folktales for All Ages (CD)
- Hold it...So That I Can Make the Bed
- Bounce Back, Too — by Diane James (with contribution by Vincent Kituku)
- Top 45 Must Know Life Lessons for Top Achievers (also available in wall poster format)
- Motivational T-Shirts With Words of Wisdom by Author/ Speaker Dr. Kituku.

Some keynotes and seminars programs offered by Kituku & Associates:

- Buffaloes in the Workplace: Thriving in Chaotic Times
- Overcoming Buffaloes as Leaders: How to Motivate Employees to Increase Productivity
- Balancing Work and Life: Moving Forward Without Leaving Your Life Behind
- Inspiring Productivity with Stories/Metaphors
- Outstanding Presentations: What You Need to Know to Give Presentations that Make People Listen, Think and Act
- How to Speak and Get Paid (Greatly)
- Living and Working with Cultural Differences